I0087363

CHAMP

The Beginning

By Larry Hillman

Text copyright 2010 by Larry Hillman

Larry Hillman
5028 19th St.
Zephyrhills, FLORIDA 33542

Interior and Front Cover Illustrations: Jennifer Savage Britton
Book layout & design: Amanda Barnhart & Beth DeLemos
The Winn Group

All rights reserved, including the right of reproduction in whole or
in part in any form.

Printed and bound in the United States of America.

ISBN: 978-0-615-43330-1

DEDICATION

Champ is dedicated to my precious children and grandchildren...and to each and every sweet lost soul needing someone to rescue them from life's dog pound. Special thanks, gratitude and love go to my wife Jeanine, my inspiration, and without whom this endeavor would not be possible.

chapter 1

Lost and Found

"That looks like a friendly man," thought the little dog as he strolled down the sidewalk. The man had a big smile on his face and a long pole with a loop on the end in his hand.

As the man got closer, his smile turned into an angry scowl. Before the little dog realized what was happening, he felt a firm thump on his head! He looked up just in time to see the man aim the pole at him a second time. The little dog quickly jumped out of the way, turned, and started running. "Faster, faster! Run faster!" he thought, as the man chased him down the sidewalk.

"I've got to do something quick," reasoned the little dog as he turned and ran down an ally between two big buildings. He hid behind a large brown dumpster, standing quietly, trying not to make a sound. He listened for the man running down the alley but could only hear the cars as they drove past. His heart pounded in his chest as he wondered, "Why is that man chasing me? Why is he trying to hit me with that pole?"

He waited anxiously for the man to reappear. Minutes passed, and his eyelids grew heavy. He eventually drifted off to sleep.

He dreamed he was snuggled in a big soft bed next to a bowl filled with mouth-watering dog food. He opened his mouth to take a bite of the delicious chow, and then...bam! Something hit him on the head, interrupting his dream.

He woke up as he was being lifted into the air by a rope around his neck. It was

choking him! He coughed, gasped for air, and let out a pitiful yelp.

"I've got you!" he heard someone say as he struggled to get away. It was the man who had been chasing him! The man dragged him down the alley. The little dog struggled, twisted, and turned, but he couldn't get away. The dogcatcher took him to a waiting truck, lifted him into the air, and shoved him into a cage. He slammed the steel door and finally removed the tight rope from the little dog's neck.

The little dog was so angry that he charged at the man, snarling and snapping his teeth. The man jumped back as the little dog slammed into the cage door. "Whoa, Killer!" said the man. "I'll have you at the pound in no time."

"The pound!" thought the little dog. "Not the pound!" He had heard stories about that terrible place! Animals were trapped in cages and not allowed to run free. Many of his friends who had gone to the pound were never heard from again. Could the rumors that they kill dogs at the pound be true? He wasn't going to let them kill him! He would fight, and that is just what he did.

When the truck came to a stop, he could hear the man walking towards him. He moved all the way to the back of the cage and crouched down to wait. The man walked up to the cage and peered inside.

"It looks like you have calmed down," the man said, as he opened the cage door.

As soon as the door was open, the little dog sprang forward and jumped toward freedom. The man caught him by his back leg in mid-air. The little dog turned and bit the man, sinking his teeth deep into the man's hand. The man yelled in pain and let go of his leg. The little dog hit the ground with a thud but jumped up and began running. The man raced after him and called for help from other men who were standing nearby.

The little dog didn't know where he

was going, but he was traveling as fast as his little legs would go. He rounded a corner.

Bang! A big net crashed down around him. He tried to bite his way out, pulling and twisting in hopes of tearing the net. Then, he was swept off his feet and into the air. He was so tangled in the net that he could barely move, but he kept trying. He didn't want to die!

Another dogcatcher carried him inside the building and down a hallway toward some large cages in the back. Other dogs barked as they walked by, and the little dog was scared. Where were they taking him? What were they going to do with him?

The man opened a cage door and put the net on the floor. He turned it over until the little dog rolled out of the net. As soon as his feet hit the floor, he turned and raced toward the cage door. Before he could get out, the man slipped out of the cage and slammed the door right in his face.

The little dog barked, snarled, and snapped at the man, as he stooped down and looked at the little dog. "You're a mean one alright. Hey, Joe, is this little fellow the big bad dog that bit you?"

The man walked over holding a white cloth over his hand. "That dog's a killer, I tell you. He's crazy. Nobody will ever adopt a crazy killer dog like that."

As the two men walked away, the little dog kept growling and snapping so he would look tough and mean. He even growled at the other dogs as they looked at him. "What are you looking at?" he snarled. "Leave me alone. I don't need any of you."

The cement floor of the cage was hard and cold as the little dog curled up in a corner and tried to go to sleep. He was lonely and scared. He had no friends and now no hope of ever being free again. Abandoned by the world, the little dog finally fell asleep.

He awoke the next morning to the sound of dogs, a lot of dogs, barking.

He had been so upset the day before that he hadn't really noticed how many dogs were all around him. It seemed they were everywhere. There were big dogs, little dogs, brown dogs, spotted dogs--just about every kind of dog you could imagine.

"Why are they all barking?" he thought. Then he noticed a man walking from cage to cage. The man opened a tiny door at the bottom of each cage and slid in a bowl of water and a bowl of dog food. The other dogs happily greeted the man and quickly began eating.

The little dog was hungry, but he wasn't sure he could trust this man. The last time someone smiled at him, he was chased, caught, and dragged to this terrible place.

When the man came to his cage, the little dog saw that it was the same man who had brought him to the pound. The man had a bandage on his hand where the little dog had bitten him. The little dog backed away from the man and began to growl. The man looked at him and said, "So, Killer, still being a tough guy, huh? Let's see how tough you are without any food until tomorrow." He slid in only a water dish and walked away.

The little dog lapped up some water, but he was really hungry. He glanced around and saw the way the other dogs were hurriedly eating, and he knew no one was going to share any of their food with him.

As he watched the other dogs, the little dog suddenly heard voices. He looked up and saw people walking from cage to cage, peering in at the dogs. The little dog heard one of them say, "Yes, you can take home any dog here as long as you pay for their shots and the cost of their food."

"Take home?" thought the little dog. "You mean someone could take me home with them?" Suddenly, the little dog had some hope of leaving this place. "Take me," he barked. "Take me!"

The group of people slowly wandered

past each cage, as the man described the dogs. When they stopped at the little dog's cage, the little dog wagged his tail and tried to look as friendly as possible.

The man with the hurt hand quickly said, "You don't want this dog. He's a bad one. Look at this nasty bite he gave me." The little dog continued to wag his tail as the people turned away from him.

Seeing them walk away made the little dog very sad. He didn't like this place. He wanted to leave.

Over the next few days, several people passed by his cage. Each time he tried his best to look friendly, and each time they walked on by as the man called him "Killer" and told the people how the little dog had bit him.

The little dog cried himself to sleep each night, wishing he had been chosen, wishing that someone would love him, feed him, care for him, and give him a place to live.

One day the little dog heard two

men talking about him. He heard them say that he wouldn't be here too much longer. He perked up his ears to listen. He was horrified at what he heard next. It seemed that dogs that were not claimed or adopted only stayed at the pound for seven days. After that they are put to sleep. The little dog knew that was a "nice" way of saying that they are killed!

Now the little dog was desperate. He didn't know how many days he had been in this place, but he knew that he was running out of time. He needed someone to pay the price of his shots and his food. He needed someone to love him and rescue him from the awful fate that loomed just ahead. What was he going to do? He couldn't pay the price. He couldn't adopt himself. He needed help!

That same day two more people arrived at the pound. And once again, the little dog was left behind. No matter how hard he tried, he couldn't get people to adopt him--not after they heard that his name was "Killer" and that he bit people. It seemed that all was lost. He just wasn't good enough to get out of this place.

Early the next morning as the man slid in his bowl of food he said, "Well Killer, today is the day. If you aren't chosen by closing time, it's curtains for you. And I'm going to do everything I can to make sure you get what you deserve for biting me."

"I'm sorry," the little dog whimpered. "Please let me go. I'm so sorry," but the man just stood up and walked away.

Several people came in that day and chose a dog to go home with them. None of them chose the little dog known as "Killer." Each time someone walked up to his cage, the man told them how crazy the little dog was and how he was a biter.

As the day passed by, the little dog began to lose all hope of being rescued. He even stopped trying to look friendly.

It wasn't working, so why bother? When people stopped by, he just curled up on the cold, lonely cement at the back of the cage. "Nobody wants a dog like me," he thought. "I grew up on the streets. I'm not house trained. I've never had a family. They think I'm crazy, and they can see that I bite just by looking at the man's hand. It's hopeless! There's no way out." With that the little dog started to cry.

"What about this one?" he heard someone say. He recognized footsteps coming his way and overheard the man retelling his infamous story. The little dog didn't even bother to look. He just stayed curled up at the back of the cage.

"Is he sick?" someone asked when the man finished his story. "He's just laying there like he is sick or something."

"I don't know," said the man. "To tell you the truth, I don't really care. He will be put to sleep within an hour, so I don't think it really matters if he is sick or not."

"Put to sleep? This little guy? You can't

do that. He doesn't deserve to die."

"Oh, yes, he does," answered the man angrily. "He's got no home and no one to love him. He even bit me!"

"I love him," said the person.

The little dog's ears perked up at those words. "That person loves me?" thought the little dog.

"But you don't want this one!" said the man. "There are plenty of good dogs in here. Why get this one? Why, he doesn't even deserve a good home! He deserves to die."

"I'll take him," said the person. "I'll pay for his food. I'll pay for his shots. I'll give him a good home and love him with all my heart."

"But...but, he doesn't deserve this." said the man, indignantly.

"I'm not doing it because he deserves it," answered the person. "I'm doing it because I love him."

By now the little dog was sitting up looking at the person. "Could it be?" he thought. "Could they really love me enough to take me out of this place and bring me home?"

"Open the door. I want to go hug my dog."

"You're crazy. He'll bite you for sure," answered the man.

Shaking his head, he slowly opened the cage door and let the person walk inside to the little dog. The stranger knelt down and called, "Here, boy."

The little dog was so overjoyed that he ran to his new owner and jumped into a snuggly lap. The person wrapped their arms around the little dog, who licked the owner's face over and over again. The little dog gave so many sloppy, wet kisses that the person had to pull him away, laughing at the little dog's excitement. He had a home. He was leaving this place. Someone had paid the price and saved him from death. He had an owner!

In a few short minutes, the little dog was walking down the sidewalk next to his new owner. Everything seemed so wonderful. The sky was brighter. The air smelled fresher. People were friendlier. He didn't remember the world being such a great place!

"Why does everything seem so new and wonderful?" he thought. Then he knew. It was because he was loved by someone. That love moved his new owner to rescue him from death, give him a good home, and care for him.

The words his new owner had said replayed in his mind. "I'm not doing it because he deserves it. I'm doing it because I love him."

He looked up at his new owner and thought, "I love you too."

chapter 2

A Home

The little dog followed his owner down the sidewalk, up some steps, and into a nice little apartment.

"This is your new home," he heard his owner say. "I hope you like it."

"Like it?" thought the little dog. "It's great!"

He followed his owner into the kitchen and watched as he opened a box and poured some dog food into a bowl. His owner sat the bowl on the floor and said, "Here you go, boy."

The little dog began to devour what tasted like the best dog food in the whole world. "Isn't it amazing how anything you do wrapped in love seems like the best?" thought the little dog.

"I can't keep calling you 'boy,'" said his owner. "I guess I better give you a name."

As the little dog continued to eat, he heard his owner going over a list of dog names. "I've got it!" said his owner. "I'll call you 'Champ.' It's the perfect name for a dog that is a champion."

"Champion?" thought the little dog. "I'm no champion. Without being rescued, I'd be dead by now. My owner is the champion."

"Come on, Champ," said his owner. "Let me show you around the place."

"Well, if you think I'm a champ, then I guess I am a champ," barked Champ as he happily raced after his new owner.

Champ followed his owner into every room in the apartment. He learned where his bed was, where his owner slept, and where the doggy door was located for when he wanted to go outside.

"I'm sorry about not having a yard for you to play in," said his owner. "This place is just temporary. One day I'll have a great big yard in the country with lots of trees and plenty of space for you to run and play."

Over the next few weeks, Champ grew to love his owner more and more. His owner went walking with him each morning. He talked to him throughout the day. He fed him, combed him, washed him, and took him to the veterinarian to make sure he didn't get sick. His owner took care of all of Champ's needs.

Once when they were walking in the park, a big ferocious Doberman charged toward Champ, growling and threatening to tear him apart. Champ yelped and fell down, waiting for the attack. "I'm a dead dog," he thought, trembling with fear. Then his owner stepped in front of the Doberman, blocking the attack on Champ.

"Get out of here!" roared his owner. The Doberman stopped, confused. Champ's owner repeated, "Get out of here!" while raising and waving a large stick. The Doberman slowly backed away.

Champ's owner knelt down and gently asked, "Are you okay, Champ?" Champ was still shaking, so his owner picked him up and hugged him tightly. "Don't worry, Champ. You can always count on me to protect you."

It felt so good being held in his owner's strong arms. All the fear of being hurt by the Doberman left, and Champ stopped shaking. "I am so glad to have someone like you taking care of me," thought Champ, as he licked his owner on the cheek.

The next day Champ and his owner went back to the park like they always did. Champ didn't even think about the Doberman. He wasn't scared. His owner was there to protect him. Champ took off running with the other dogs, jumping and barking and having fun. After a few minutes, he ran back towards the bench where his owner always waited. As he neared the bench, he didn't see his owner. He stopped and looked all around the park.

Champ couldn't believe his eyes! His owner was petting the Doberman-- the same Doberman who tried to hurt Champ the day before. Champ stood and watched as his owner scratched behind the dog's ears and even offered him a doggy treat.

Champ didn't know what to do. How could his owner be so nice to a dog that was so mean? Champ stood silently-- not even wagging his tail-- as his owner walked over to him. Bending down, the owner said, "You must always be kind to others Champ, even those who are not kind to you."

Champ had never heard of anything like that before. He had always been kind to those who were kind to him. Anyone who was mean to him got treated just as mean in return. "I'll have to think about this," thought Champ.

What Champ saw his owner doing at the park the following day was even more unbelievable! His owner was giving treats to a group of dogs. They were not just any dogs. These were stray dogs, dogs that were dirty and smelly. They were dogs that ate out of trash cans and licked up food spilled on dirty sidewalks and streets, dogs that nobody loved. They were the same dogs that other owners at the park chased away because they didn't want their own dogs to be around those kinds of dogs. His owner was treating them like they were special, like they were clean and didn't smell.

The next day at the park, and everyday thereafter, Champ saw his owner talking to and helping many people and dogs. Some of them looked old, some young, some nice, and some mean. It was as if what they looked like didn't matter. His owner was nice to everyone.

Champ still wasn't too sure about this being nice to everyone stuff. It seemed to work for his owner, but he wasn't so sure it would work for him. That is until one day when he came face to face with the Doberman. Champ had run after a stick that his owner had thrown behind some big trees. As he ran around one tree, he tripped over something and rolled to a stop. When he looked to see what he had tripped over, it was the Doberman. The Doberman sat up and yawned. Champ had interrupted his nap.

"Oh, great!" thought Champ. "He's going to be really mad at me now." But instead of barking wildly or trying to bite him, the Doberman just looked at him.

"Your owner is very nice," barked the Doberman. "You are a lucky dog." Then the Doberman stood up and walked away.

"Wow!" thought Champ. "He didn't hurt me."

A voice came from behind him, "Being kind to others always pays off, doesn't it?" Champ turned around to see his owner standing behind another tree. "Being kind to the Doberman the other day really helped you out, didn't it? Just think what could have happened if I had been mean to him!"

"It works!" thought Champ. "It really works." Right then and there, Champ decided that he would act just like his owner. He would be kind to everyone, even those who were not kind to him.

The next day at the park, Champ met some new friends, Rex and Rover. They had just moved to town, and Champ decided to be kind to them. As they ran and played in the park, he noticed that they were a little rougher than the other dogs. Rex and Rover would knock other dogs down as they went after a ball, and they even got into a fight over a stick that one of the owners had thrown. Champ continued to be kind, just like his owner had taught him.

That night as Champ lay curled up on his owner's lap, his owner began talking about the new dogs Champ had met. "Champ," said his owner, "I saw you playing with some new friends today. I liked the way that you were kind to them."

Champ wagged his tail showing that he liked being complimented.

"I want you to keep on being kind to them and always treat them nicely. But I also want you to be careful. Those dogs are pretty rough, and I don't want you to start acting like them. I noticed that they have some bad habits that I don't want you to pick up."

Champ wagged his tail again and thought, "No problem."

Day after day Champ continued to play with his new friends. His owner often suggested that he play with some other dogs, but Champ always ended up playing with Rex and Rover.

One day as they chased a ball that had gone behind some bushes, Rex barked, "Hey Rover, look at that. It's a butcher shop."

"Yeah," answered Rover, "and the side door is open. I bet we could sneak in there and get something to eat."

"What do you say, Champ? Are you with us?" asked Rex.

Suddenly, Champ felt sick in his stomach, and he couldn't speak. He stood there frozen in place, looking at Rex and Rover.

"Come on, Champ. You're not scared, are you?" snarled Rex. "Don't worry about our owners. They will never know. These bushes will hide us from their view."

Champ's owner had always warned him to never leave the park. His owner also gave him all the food he wanted, so he did not need to take any from the butcher.

As Rex and Rover kept talking to him, he found himself sneaking out of the park, across the street, and into the butcher shop's side door.

Just as Rover had suggested, there was plenty to eat inside the shop. Champ's heart was beating so fast that

he thought it might burst. He stood just inside the door and watched as Rex and Rover picked up large pieces of meat and headed for the door. Champ turned to follow them just as the butcher rounded the corner.

"Come back here!" the butcher hollered. The butcher ran toward the dogs shouting, "Bring that back!"

Champ didn't have to be told to run. He was so scared that his legs took off running before his brain even thought about it. Champ followed Rex and Rover across the street and into the trees. The butcher ran out into the street before stopping. He couldn't leave his store unattended, so he shook his head and returned to his shop.

Rex and Rover quickly ate the meat that they had stolen and began to brag about what they had done. Champ laughed along with them as they talked about how funny the butcher looked running after them and how funny he sounded yelling, "Stop!" and

"Bring that back!"

Champ was having so much fun that he lost track of time. The sun was sinking below the tree line. Champ said goodbye to Rex and Rover and searched for his owner. His owner was walking through the park, calling his name.

"Where have you been?" said his owner. "I've been looking for you everywhere." Champ barked and jumped into his owner's arms. "I thought you might have gotten hurt or lost," said his owner.

Just then Rex and Rover came running past on their way home.

"So that's it," said Champ's owner, disapprovingly. "You were with Rex and Rover." Champ continued to kiss his owner's face as his owner said, "Champ, I think it would be a good thing if you stayed away from Rex and Rover. I don't think they are a very good influence on you."

Champ stopped licking his owner's face. He couldn't believe what he was hearing! Those guys were his friends. They had lots of fun together.

"I know you think they are your friends, but you don't need friends like them. Listen to me, Champ. I love you and don't want anything bad to happen to you. If you keep hanging around with Rex and Rover, it will only get you into trouble."

"Nothing bad will happen," barked Champ. "I won't get into any trouble."

chapter 3

Let's have some fun.

The next day Champ played with the other dogs just to make his owner happy. However, as soon as he was out of sight, he ran to where Rex and Rover were playing. As he walked up, Rex barked, "Hey Champ, we are sneaking out tonight. We want to run wild and free around town without our owners. It's going to be a blast. Why don't you join us?"

"Sneak out?" asked Champ. "What do you mean...'sneak out'?"

"You know, wait until your owner is asleep, and then go out through your doggy door. You do have a doggy door, don't you?"

"Well, sure," said Champ, "but I've never gone farther than the front yard of the apartment building. Besides, I don't think my owner would like me running around town at night."

"Why do you think we are sneaking out?" answered Rover. "We don't want our owners to know. They don't want us to have any fun, so we sneak out without them knowing it."

"What time does your owner go to sleep?" asked Rex.

"Around 10:00," answered Champ.

"We will be at your place around 10:30. Just crawl through the doggy door as usual, and then wait for us on your steps."

With that Rex and Rover ran off saying, "We'll see you later."

As he walked home with his owner, Champ was deep in thought. He wasn't sure what he was going to do. If he didn't go, Rex and Rover would make fun of him and maybe stop being his friends. If he did go and his owner found out, well, he didn't know what would happen.

Champ's thinking was interrupted as his owner picked him up and said, "You sure are being quiet. Is something bothering you?"

Champ wagged his tail and licked his owner's cheek.

"I know what it is," said his owner. "It's those two dogs you've been playing with at the park. Look what they've done to you? Imagine how quiet and distant you will be if you keep hanging around them?"

Champ's owner looked into Champ's eyes and said, "Champ, do not hang around those dogs any more. They are not good for you. They are trying to get you to be like them, and sooner or later, something bad will happen. I think you should stay away from them. From now on, when we go to the park, you must play by the benches where I sit. You can't go running into the trees where the other dogs play."

"They were right," thought Champ. "Rex and Rover were right! My owner doesn't want me to have any fun. Well, that does it! I'm sneaking out tonight and having some fun!"

Champ curled up in his bed just like he did every evening after his owner said goodnight. He listened quietly as his owner got into bed and turned out the light. He lay there in the darkness considering what he was about to do. What if something bad did happen? What if he got lost and couldn't find his way home? What if he got caught by that awful man again and taken back to the pound?

Suddenly, out of the darkness, he heard a voice, "Are you coming or not?"

Champ raised his head to see Rex peeking in through the doggy door.

"Come on! Let's go!" whispered Rex, impatiently.

Champ stood up and began creeping towards the door. He had never been so scared in his whole life. He poked his head out of the doggy door to see Rex, Rover, and three other dogs standing on the sidewalk.

"Hurry it up, would ya? We haven't got all night," growled Rover.

Champ walked out on the sidewalk and stood next to the other dogs.

"Who are these guys?" he asked.

"They are strays that we met down by the city dump a little while ago. They call themselves 'The Trashy Trio,' since they dig in the trash all day. Funny stuff, huh?" laughed Rover.

"Oh, real funny," said Champ, forcing a smile and trying to act calm.

"Follow me!" shouted Rex, as he turned and raced down the sidewalk.

Champ ran after him with the other dogs. He knew what he was doing was wrong. He wished he had never come outside. It was too late; the other dogs wouldn't let him turn back now. He was running with a pack of wild dogs, and he had no idea where they were going.

Before long they were knocking over trash cans, chasing cats, digging up flower beds, and howling under windows until the homeowners turned on the lights. They ran from street to street making as much noise and mess as possible. Each time someone yelled at them or threw something their way, the dogs ran off laughing and howling. They ran up onto the back steps of houses and ate food set out for the dogs that lived in those homes. If a dog tried to stop them, they just beat him up and took the food anyway. After all, it was six dogs to one, and they could easily overpower any dog that resisted. Actually, it was mostly five dogs to one. Champ just couldn't bring himself to hurt a dog protecting his food or property.

"This is great, isn't it?" smiled Rex.

The Trashy Trio answered in unison, "Yes it is!" Everyone laughed.

"But, it isn't funny," thought Champ

to himself. "These people are trying to sleep, and who will clean up the mess we keep making?"

"All for one and one for all! Right, guys?" said Rover. "Through thick and thin, we will always be together. If one of us is in trouble, all of us will help. What do you say, guys? Put 'er there," said Rover, as he stuck out his paw.

All of the other dogs put their paws on top of Rover's, including Champ.

"This is kind of neat," thought Champ, forgetting about all the trouble they caused. "I've never been a part of a group like this before."

As the pack ran down the street, it was hard for Champ to keep up. He was much shorter than the other dogs and couldn't run as fast. Before long, the others began to tease him about being slow. It was funny to them, but Champ really didn't like it.

Then, as the pack turned down a dark alley, Champ got lost. At least, he thought he had gotten lost. He rounded a corner and didn't see any of the other dogs. He stopped and looked up and down the alley, but his friends were nowhere in sight. He began to walk slowly down the dark, creepy alley. Then, before he knew it, something bit his back leg, and a loud noise scared him half to death. He let out a loud yelp and took off running down the alley.

When he got to the end of the alley, he noticed that the noise had stopped, and, instead, he heard laughing. He looked back, and there were his so-called friends. They were pointing at him with one paw and holding their stomachs with the other as they rolled with laughter.

Champ was furious. He didn't know whether to cry or scream. One thing was for sure. He was going to get even with those guys. He took off running at the pack with fire in his eyes. The others saw him coming and started to run. Champ chased them into an abandoned building. He couldn't see them, but he heard them running into the next room. He charged around a corner after them.

All of a sudden, Champ tripped over a trash can and fell into a shallow hole in the floor. He landed in cold slimy liquid that stuck to his fur. He wiped his eyes with his paws but the gooey stuff just smeared across his face.

"I told you it would work," laughed one of The Trashy Trio. "We've done it a hundred times. All you have to do is get one of these stupid little dogs mad, and they will run into that big hole full of engine oil every single time."

"See ya around, stupid!" said Rover as he and the others ran away laughing. They left Champ all by himself, sitting in a pool of dirty motor oil. Champ tried to follow them, but his oily paws just slipped and slid on the floor.

Champ gave up and watched as they ran away into the night. "Some friends they are," he thought. Champ wondered what had happened to "all for one and one for all."

He looked around the old garage for something to wipe off the oil. It was hard to see in the dark, but he did find some old newspaper. He managed to wipe the oil out of his eyes and off his paws.

Champ wandered into the street. It was after midnight, and the dim street lights revealed a deserted street with no traffic. Champ was dirty, smelly, cold, embarrassed, ashamed, angry, and scared — all at the same time. Most of all, he was lost. He didn't have any idea where he was. He had just followed the others without paying attention. He had trusted them to show him the way home. Now he realized that they had planned this all along. They wanted to get him lost.

"And I trusted those guys," thought Champ. "I thought they were my friends. My owner was right. He said that something bad would happen if I hung around with those dogs, and now it has. I'm lost, sleepy, hungry, cold, wet, oily, dirty, and smelly. I don't know how to get home, or where I can sleep the rest of the night. Oh, why didn't I listen to my owner?"

Champ found an old blanket behind a dumpster in the alley. He curled up on the blanket and tried to fall asleep. Maybe he could find his way home in the morning. He sure missed his nice warm bed. Champ cried himself to sleep, whimpering over and over, "Why didn't I listen? Why didn't I listen?"

The next morning Champ wandered the streets, looking for a way home. People pointed at him as he passed by, and many of them chased him away from their front doors as he stopped to smell the food inside. Even the stray dogs didn't want him around. Many of them laughed at him, and others cruelly told him to go away. No one offered to help Champ — no food, no water, no kindness at all.

Champ began digging through smelly old garbage cans trying to find something to eat. He had to lick up water from

puddles on the street. The water tasted like motor oil, but it was all he had. He spent another night behind a dumpster, this time under some old newspaper. All night long he dreamed of his owner, his home, his bed, and plenty of food. Each time that he woke up in the cold wind, he realized that it was all a dream. He had lost it all by doing something dumb and stupid. Even if he did find his way home, his owner probably wouldn't want him back. Who would want a dog that was covered with grease and oil, who was smelly, and, most of all, who didn't obey his owner?

The next day Champ again roamed the streets. This time he was just looking for something to eat. Once, as he ran between cars crossing the street, he thought he heard someone call his name. He didn't have time to stop and look while in the street. Besides, no one called him "Champ" but his owner.

Later that day he heard his name called again. He turned around to see the source. What he saw made him feel worse than anything in his whole life. It was Rex and Rover. They were both sticking their heads out of the rear window of their owner's car. "You need a bath. I can smell you way over here," sneered Rover.

"You look hungry," laughed Rex.

"See you some other time, Chump, I mean Champ!" they snickered as the car drove away.

Champ had never been so sad in his whole life--not even when he had been taken away from his mother or when he was locked up in the pound. Champ sat right there on the sidewalk and began to cry.

"Nobody loves me," he sobbed. "Nobody cares if I live or die."

Again he heard his named called, but he wasn't going to look up and let Rex and Rover see him crying."I could die out here on the street. What if I get caught and go back to the pound?" he whined.

Again he heard his name called. This time the voice was closer, and it didn't sound like Rex or Rover.

Champ lifted his head. Through the tears in his eyes, he saw someone running down the side walk. He blinked the tears away and tried to get a better look. Could it be? No, it couldn't. Still, it was! It was his owner! Champ stood up and, without thinking, began to run toward his owner. As he ran he remembered what had happened. Would his owner want him back? After all, he was dirty, smelly, and had run away.

Before Champ could wonder anymore, his owner picked him up and gave him the biggest, tightest hug he had ever had. The grease and oil didn't seem to matter. The dirty smell didn't seem to matter either.

"Oh Champ!" said his owner. "I've been looking all over for you. I missed you so much."

His owner still loved him! His owner still cared!

"How did you get so dirty?" asked his owner. "I'd better get you home and cleaned up."

Champ's owner held him in his arms all the way home. Never before had Champ felt so much love. He knew where he belonged. He knew he was special. He curled up tight in his owner's arms and rested.

That evening as Champ lay in his bed, he thought about the past few days. He thought about how his so-called friends were not his friends at all. He thought about how lonely it was being out on the streets all alone. He thought about how his owner had warned him, and how he had not listened. He thought about all the bad things that could have happened to him. He also thought about what a big lie Rex and Rover had told him when they said his owner didn't want him to have any fun. The last few days could be called a lot of things, but "fun" was not one of them. No, his owner wasn't trying to stop him from having fun; his owner was protecting him from being hurt. As he snuggled against his nice warm pillow, Champ promised himself that next time, he would listen to and obey his owner.

The End

www.ingramcontent.com/pod-product-compliance
Lightning Source LLC
Chambersburg PA
CBHW071431040426
42445CB00012BA/1341